To Calen,

From your Parents

histories PRESENTS

CHRISTOPHER COWLUMBUS

Based on the life of the great explorer, Christopher Columbus

Written and Illustrated by:
ANDREW TOFFOLI

Color Design by:
MARIA GONZALEZ

CHRISTOPHER COWLUMBUS
Copyright © **The Little Germ That Could... Creations**, 2004

All Rights Reserved

Printed in China

ISBN 978-0-976-3233-0-3

Library of Congress Control Number: 2008905418

**Our mission is to educate children about history
while using humor and imagination to teach valuable life lessons.**

Please visit us online at **www.littlegerm.com**

10 9 8 7 6 5 4 3 2 1

For Penny

Christopher Cowlumbus was a daydreaming, adventurous bovine that was born in Genoa, Italy in 1452.

Chris loved to read about sailors from far away places.

Chris worked in a bookstore where he would help sailors buy maps for their journeys.

While in the store, the sailors would tell Chris stories about their exciting trips.

This made Chris daydream about exploring exotic lands and finding hidden treasure.

But Chris knew that sailing trips cost a lot...

Upset by this,
Chris thought...

...and thought

... and thought until he came up with who had the most money around.

He shouted,
"The King and Queen of Spain are my ticket to fame!"

Chris arrived and met the King and Queen and respectfully asked for a donation.

The King and Queen thought about it...

...and thought about it

...and thought about it

...and thought about it

...and came up with the answer...

Chris was not happy with their answer.

Several years had passed, and Chris was still upset.

He could not stop dreaming about his trip.

So one day he got tired of only dreaming and ran back to Spain.

The Queen listened to what Chris had to say.

"I need to sail.
And with your help,
I will not fail."

...and thought

...and thought

...and thought

...and thought about h
request and finally said

"Yes."

Chris replied, "Yes?...
Did you say yes?!"

Chris ran into town cheering...
"Yes... she said YES!!"

So in 1492 the Niña, Pinta and Santa Mooria set sail.

Chris proudly sailed his ship through the open blue waters.

So the ships sailed on with no direction and no land in sight.

Chris was about to give up and turn around until he spotted birds in the sky.

And soon enough...
atop of the ship a crewman
could see land ahead.

Chris then anchored his ships, gathered gifts and took a small boat to reach the shore.

As the crew rowed, the land became closer...

... and closer

...until they reached the sandy shore.

It was not long before someone came out to greet the visitors.

Chris uttered to the natives...
"I hope these gifts are enough, for you to welcome us."

The chief replied...
"Of course you are welcome here. Sailing is an amazing feat for a steer!"

The natives were amazed at the gifts Chris brought.

But after weeks of fun and discovery...

It was time to sail home.

So the Niña, Pinta and Santa Mooria left the island and headed home.

Chris returned to Spain and brought back presents to a very proud Queen.

Everybody cheered and celebrated Chris' return.

Christopher Cowlumbus changed the world and proved what you can do if you never give up on your dreams.

COMING SOON! from hi·stories PRESENTS®

Thomas Owlva Edison™

Thomouse Jefferson™

Marco Hippolo™

Paw-l Revere™

Bark Twain™

All artwork and characters are protected under U.S copyright laws. Copyright 2009, The Little Germ That Could... Creations